FRANCE

Marshall Cavendish
Benchmark

New York

Written by: Fiona Conboy/Roseline Ngcheong-Lum
Editors: Peter Mavrikis, Cheryl Sim
Publisher: Michelle Bisson
Series Designer: Benson Tan

Photo research by Thomas Khoo

Originated and designed by Marshall Cavendish International (Asia) Pte Ltd
Copyright © 2011 Marshall Cavendish International (Asia) Pte Ltd
Published by Marshall Cavendish Benchmark
An imprint of Marshall Cavendish Corporation
All rights reserved.

No part of this publication may be reproduced, stored in a retrieval system
or transmitted, in any form or by any means, electronic, mechanical,
photocopying, recording, or otherwise, without the prior permission of the
copyright owner. Request for permission should be addressed to the Publisher,
Marshall Cavendish Corporation, 99 White Plains Road, Tarrytown, NY 10591.
Tel: (914) 332-8888, fax: (914) 332-1888.
Website: www.marshallcavendish.us

This publication represents the opinions and views of the authors based on
Fiona Conboy and Roseline Ngcheong-Lum's personal experience, knowledge,
and research. The information in this book serves as a general guide only.
The authors and publisher have used their best efforts in preparing this
book and disclaim liability rising directly and indirectly from the use and
application of this book.

Other Marshall Cavendish Offices:
Marshall Cavendish International (Asia) Private Limited, 1 New Industrial Road,
Singapore 536196 ● Marshall Cavendish International (Thailand) Co Ltd.
253 Asoke, 12th Flr, Sukhumvit 21 Road, Klongtoey Nua, Wattana,
Bangkok 10110, Thailand ● Marshall Cavendish (Malaysia) Sdn Bhd,
Times Subang, Lot 46, Subang Hi-Tech Industrial Park, Batu Tiga,
40000 Shah Alam, Selangor Darul Ehsan, Malaysia

Marshall Cavendish is a trademark of Times Publishing Limited.
All websites were available and accurate when this book was sent to press.

Library of Congress Cataloging-in-Publication Data
Conboy, Fiona.
France / Fiona Conboy and Roseline Ngcheong-Lum.
p. cm. — (Welcome to my country)
Summary: "An overview of the history, geography, government, economy,
language, people, and culture of France. Includes numerous color photos,
useful facts, and a detailed map and resource section"
—Provided by publisher.
Includes index.
ISBN 978-1-60870-153-7
1. France—Juvenile literature.
I. NgCheong-Lum, Roseline, 1962-   II. Title.
DC17.C66 2011
944—dc22   2010006357

Printed in Malaysia
135642

PHOTO CREDITS
Alamy Images: 1, 3 (top), 4, 15 (middle), 16 (left), 28, 31 (top)
alt.TYPE/Reuters: 17
Bes Stock: 36 (top)
Corbis: 5, 34
Focus Team Italy: 2, 18, 27, 32, 37
Getty Images: 16 (right), 31 (bottom)
Haga Library: 38
HBL Network Photo Agency: 3 (bottom), 10, 15 (bottom), 19 (bottom),
    24 (both), 25, 40
Hutchison Library: 23, 43
Illustrated London News Picture Library: 14, 29 (left)
Musée des Beaux-Arts, Tournai: 3 (bottom), 30 (top)
North Wind Picture Archives: 12, 15 (top), 29 (right)
Photolibrary: cover, 6, 7, 8, 9,11 (both), 13, 22, 26, 30 (bottom), 33,
    35, 36 (botttom), 39, 41, 45
Trip Photographic Library: 19 (top)

Contents

Words that appear in the glossary are printed in **boldface** type the first time they occur in the text.

Many quaint villages can be found in the French countryside.

Welcome to France!

The largest nation in western Europe, France has been a leader in the arts for many centuries. It is also a country of contrasts. Its culture combines traditional values and modern style. Let's explore the land of delicious **cuisine** and elegant fashions and learn more about the French!

The Arch de Triomphe is one of the most popular landmarks in France.

The Flag of France

The French flag is made up of blue, white, and red panels. It is called the Tricolor. Blue and red are the colors of France's capital city, Paris. White was the color of the kings of France between 1638 and 1790.

The Land

France covers an area of 212,742 square miles (551,000 square kilometers) in Europe. Various overseas territories in the Mediterranean Sea, the Caribbean Sea, the Pacific Ocean, the Indian Ocean, and the Atlantic Ocean also belong to France.

The Massif Central, a large, granite **plateau**, makes up one-sixth of the country. The plateau is lined with deep gorges and is dotted with extinct volcanoes, crater lakes, and hot mineral springs, including the resort town of Vichy.

The French Alps stretch along the border with Switzerland and Italy in southeastern France. Mont Blanc, in the French Alps, is the highest peak in France at 15,771 feet (4,805 meters).

In the days before cars, trains, and planes, rivers and canals formed an important transportation and communications network for the different regions in France.

Mountainous regions form France's borders with Italy in the southeast and Spain in the south. One of these, the French Alps, boasts many popular ski resorts. The highest peaks there are called the Massif du Mont Blanc.

France is famous for its rivers, which include the Seine, the Rhône, and the Rhine. For centuries, the French crossed the country by boat on these rivers.

Climate

The French climate varies greatly from region to region. The French Riviera is warm, while the mountain areas are colder. In the northwest, the Atlantic Ocean brings wet weather.

Alsace often experiences snowfall during the cold winter months.

8

Storks migrate to France from Africa during the summer months. They build their nests in treetops and on the roofs of buildings.

Plants and Animals

Forests cover about one quarter of France. Wild animals, such as snakes, brown bears, wolves, and deer, live in the forests and national parks, while antelope roam the mountains.

The coastal areas are home to a variety of birds and sea creatures. Efforts by the National Forestry Office have increased the amount of forested areas since 1945.

History

Gaul and the Roman Empire

The **Celts** (KELTS) were the first to invade France, which was earlier known as Gaul. In 52 BCE, the Roman general Julius Caesar defeated the Gaul chief Vercingetorix. For the next 500 years, the Romans ruled Gaul. In the fifth century, Germanic tribes invaded and conquered the Romans.

The defeated Celtic leader Vercingetorix lays down his weapons before the Roman general —and future emperor—Julius Caesar.

The Middle Ages

During a period known as the **Middle Ages**, France was the most powerful kingdom in western Europe. In 1337, France and England fought each other in the Hundred Years' War. With the help of a young woman, Joan of Arc, the French army saved France from English occupation.

The English were about to conquer France when Joan of Arc led French troops to victory at Orleans in 1429. She was named a saint in 1920, almost 500 years after her death.

Renaissance and Reformation

The **Renaissance** came to France from Italy in the fifteenth century. It was a time of scholarly learning in Europe.

In the sixteenth century, the **Reformation** created the Protestant Church in France. Catholics and Protestants fought each other for many years.

During the seventeenth century, Louis XIV ruled France. Said to be one of the greatest kings of France, he encouraged the French to explore the land now known as North America.

Louis XIV, also known as the Sun King, was said to glow with a glorious light. Classical art and literature flourished during his reign.

On July 14, 1789, a mob of angry peasants stormed the Bastille, a prison in Paris. Throughout the land, castles were invaded and destroyed by commoners who were unhappy with the privileges bestowed on the French **aristocracy**.

The French Revolution

In 1789, conflicts between French commoners and the nobility led to the French Revolution. This struggle lasted for ten years. In 1792, the **monarchy** was abolished, and King Louis XVI and his wife, Marie Antoinette, were found guilty of **treason**. They were executed.

During the revolution, an officer named Napoleon Bonaparte rose to power. In 1799, he formed a new government. France soon went to war against the rest of Europe. Napoleon became emperor but was eventually defeated by other European armies.

By the early 1900s, France and Britain had become **allies**. Russia and Britain defended France from the Germans during World War I (1914–1918). Almost 2 million French soldiers died during the war. The United States, which entered the war in 1917, helped France drive the Germans out and win back conquered territories.

The Arc de Triomphe in Paris was built to celebrate the victories of Napoleon. After each of the world wars, troops marched through the Arc in triumph. A national remembrance service is held there each year to honor those who lost their lives in battle.

World War II

In 1939, Nazi Germany invaded Poland, and Britain and France declared war against the Germans. The Germans invaded Paris in 1940 and divided the country into two regions. The northern half of France was occupied by the Nazis, while a puppet government was established in the south that was loyal to the Germans. During World War II, General Charles de Gaulle led a French rebel group, the Resistance, against the Germans. In 1944, British, American, and Canadian soldiers landed in France and freed it from German occupation. World War II formally ended in 1945.

Charles de Gaulle's goal after World War II was to make France the leader of Europe.

After the War

In 1959, Charles de Gaulle became president of France. However, some of the French were dissatisfied with his government. In the 1960s, university students organized a series of **demonstrations** against the way the country was run. The French government survived by making widespread **reforms**. Today, France holds a strong position in world affairs.

Charlemagne (742—814)

Charlemagne, or Charles the Great, ruled France from 768 to 814. In 800, he was crowned emperor of a vast region that included most of western Europe.

Charlemagne

Marie Antoinette (1755—1793)

Marie Antoinette was not a popular queen—particularly with the poorer people of France. When she heard that the peasants did not have any bread, she told them to eat cake instead, marking her ignorance at the plight of the poor.

Marie Antoinette

Napoleon Bonaparte (1769—1821)

Napoleon led France in wars against the rest of western Europe in the late 1700s and early 1800s. He was defeated in 1815. He developed the Napoleonic Code for France, a series of laws that forms the basis of French law today.

Napoleon Bonaparte

The Government and the Economy

France is a **republic** led by a **democratically** elected president. The president makes important decisions about national and foreign affairs. He or she also appoints the prime minister, who looks after the day-to-day running of the country.

France's twenty-two regions are divided into ninety-six departments, each run by a local council and an official from the main government.

Nicolas Sarkozy (**left**) has been president of France since 2007. Francois Fillon (**right**) has been Sarkozy's prime minister since 2007.

The National Assembly meets to debate national and international issues.

Elections

Two houses—the National Assembly and the Senate—make up the French parliament. Every French citizen over the age of eighteen has the right to vote for a president and members of parliament. Citizens also vote for their local councils.

National Service

Until 2001, all French males between the ages of eighteen and thirty-five were required to serve in the army, navy, or air force for one year.

Fishermen in Brittany bring ashore many types of fresh seafood.

Agriculture

France has one of the world's strongest economies. Agriculture is an important sector. France produces crops, such as wheat, corn, sugar beet, and grapes.

France is well-known for its fine wines as well as delicious dairy products, such as milk, cheese, and cream. French beef and veal are exported to other European countries. In the northern part of France, the fishing industry thrives.

An Economic Leader

France has become a world leader in technology. Besides cars, satellites, and telecommunications equipment, France manufactures advanced civilian and military aircraft and high-speed trains, such as the TGV.

France was one of the founding members of the **European Union** (EU), a group of European countries with strong economic ties and a common currency. France trades with other EU countries, as well as with the United States, Japan, and Russia.

Grape pickers at work at a vineyard on the outskirts of Nice, in the southeast of France.

The fastest passenger plane in the world was the Concorde, made by Air France and British Airways. It reached speeds of 1,330 miles (2,140 kilometers) per hour. After twenty-seven years, the Concorde was withdrawn from service in 2003.

People and Lifestyle

More than 60 million people live in France. Their diverse appearance reflects the many groups—Alpine, Nordic, and Mediterranean—from which they descend. People from many different parts of the world have settled in France and made it their home. During the last hundred years, **immigrants** have arrived from central and eastern Europe, Africa, the Middle East, and Asia.

A large number of North African immigrants live in France.

Friends and family share in the fun during a big Bastille Day picnic. The French love spending leisure time together.

Social Classes

There is a strong social structure in France. Many people in the upper class, or aristocracy, live in the grand homes of their ancestors. However, they no longer have the power their families once held. The middle class, or *bourgeoisie* (boor-zhwah-ZEE), is the largest and most influential group. Most professionals belong to this group. Farmers and manual workers form the working class. The distinction between the middle and working classes is diminishing.

Rural Life

Life in the French countryside is quiet. After World War II, many villagers moved to towns and cities to look for jobs. As a result, many rural houses are now used as vacation homes. For the people who still live in the countryside, social and leisure activities usually center on the village square.

Large tracts of land are designated for agriculture. Most farmers use tractors to work their fields.

The streets of Paris always bustle with shoppers and tourists.

City Life

Approximately 2 million people live in Paris, which is one of
the most densely populated cities in the world. Other major
cities are Lyon, Marseille, Bordeaux, and Lille. Impressive
old buildings, once the homes of the aristocracy, are found
in most city centers. Today, they function as offices or small
apartments but retain their elegance and charm. Homes in the
city center are expensive, so most people live in the **suburbs**.
French families, especially those in the cities, tend to be small.

Women

In the late nineteenth century, French women began the fight for women's rights in their country. In 1945, women were given the right to vote. Today, they enjoy legal equality with men. One of the most famous French women is Marie Curie. Her scientific work on radioactivity paved the way for cancer treatment. France's first female prime minister was Edith Cresson, elected in 1991.

Scientists Marie and Pierre Curie studied radioactivity. In 1906, Marie Curie became the first woman to be appointed professor at the Sorbonne University in Paris.

More and more women in France work in jobs outside the home.

In addition to their regular school lessons, young French students sometimes take classes in music, dance, and art.

Education

The **literacy rate** in France is high—99.2 percent of adults can read and write. Schooling is free and required for children between the ages of six and sixteen. Primary school lasts for six years and is followed by four years of secondary school. Three years of *lycée* (li-SAY), or high school, follow secondary school, after which the top students attend a university.

Christianity

Until the French Revolution of 1789–1799, the official religion of France was Roman Catholicism. After the Revolution, France was declared simply "Christian." Today, more than 80 percent of the population is Christian—mainly Roman Catholic. However, less than 10 percent of this number attend church regularly.

The altar of the Notre-Dame de la Garde in Marseille, which was built in the 1850s. The church is in the Neo-Byzantine style, a form of architecture that was popular in Europe in the nineteenth century when building churches and cathedrals.

Paris has a diverse population representing a variety of religions.

Islam

After Christianity, Islam is the second largest religion in France. Many Muslims originally came from North Africa. Today, Muslims make up about 7 to 10 percent of the population.

Judaism

One percent of the population is Jewish. Today, there are more Jews in France than in any other country in western Europe.

Language

The French language is derived from Latin. Romans brought it to Gaul in 52 BCE. Before this, the Gauls spoke Celtic languages. Between the ninth and fourteenth centuries, two **dialects** were spoken—*langue d'oc* (LAHNG dohk) in the north, and *langue d'oïl* (LAHNG doy) in the south. The northern dialect was adopted as the common language. Today, more than 250 million people in the world speak French.

Traditional book stands, like this one, are commonly found in street markets. Most of the books sold are in French.

(**Left**) Victor Hugo (1802–1855) wrote *Les Miserables,* a novel based on the French Revolution. (**Right**) Aurore Dudevant (1804–1876) wrote novels and short stories under the pen name "George Sand."

Literature

France has produced some of the greatest writers of all time. Their works are studied throughout the world.

Classical plays by Pierre Corneille, Jean Racine, and Jean-Baptiste Molière charmed King Louis XIV and his court.

During the nineteenth century, Victor Hugo wrote *The Hunchback of Notre Dame*, and Alexandre Dumas penned *The Three Musketeers*. Other French literary greats include Marcel Proust, Jean Paul Sartre, Albert Camus, Simone de Beauvoir, and Hélène Cixous. In 2008, Jean-Marie Gustave Le Clézio, who is regarded as one of Europe's greatest authors, received the Nobel Prize in Literature.

Arts

Painting

Over 15,000 years ago, prehistoric artists created the world's first paintings in caves in France.

In the nineteenth century, artists of the impressionist movement used color and light to portray people and landscapes as they looked at particular times of the day. Claude Monet's painting, *Impression: Sunrise*, gave this artistic style its name. Another famous impressionist painter is Édouard Manet.

Argentueil, 1874, by painter Édouard Manet.

Visitors to the Louvre, an art museum in Paris, enter through this glass pyramid.

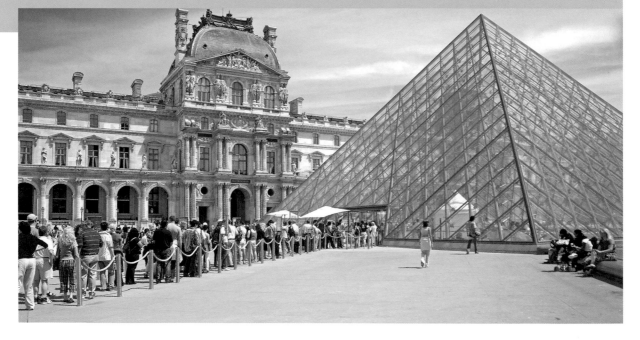

Film

Drawing on American Thomas Edison's inventions, Frenchmen Louis and Auguste Lumière invented the film projector in the nineteenth century.

Today, France produces hundreds of films every year, from comedy to drama. Each year the best new films from all around the world are screened at the Cannes Fim Festival. In 2008, French director Laurent Cantent won the prestigious Palm d'Or (Golden Palm) at Cannes for his film *Entre les Murs* (*The Class*). Jean Reno, Gérard Depardieu, Audrey Tatou, and Marion Cotillard are French film stars who have enjoyed success in Hollywood.

In 2007, Marion Cotillard became the first person to win an Academy Award for Best Actress in a French-speaking role.

Fashion

During the twentieth century, Paris established itself as the fashion capital of the world. Gabrielle "Coco" Chanel, Christian Dior, Yves Saint Laurent, and Jeanne Lanvin became famous for designing exclusive custom-made clothing, also known as *haute couture* (oht koo-TYR). Their names have become brands that remain highly popular today.

Coco Chanel modernized women's wear and was also the first designer to produce her own perfume, Chanel No. 5.

Architecture

The changing tastes of the French are reflected in the country's many architectural styles. The dramatic **Gothic** style developed between the twelfth and sixteenth centuries. The Renaissance followed, and fine castles and churches appeared across France.

The spectacular Palace of Versailles in Paris was built during the reign of King Louis XIV. France's most famous structure, the Eiffel Tower, was built for the World's Fair in 1889.

Notre Dame Cathedral is a magnificent example of Gothic architecture. It features stained-glass windows and tall, elaborate spires.

The lace headdress is part of the traditional **Breton** garments that are normally worn during the Festival de Cournouaille in Brittany.

Lace-Making

Brittany, in northwestern France, is one of the few regions where lace-making still thrives. Lace-making and other traditional crafts are practiced in many French towns and villages.

Leisure Time

The Great Outdoors

The French love to spend their leisure time outdoors. The changing landscape provides great spots for a variety of activities, including hiking, climbing, cycling, horseriding, and skiing.

Many French city dwellers have second homes in the countryside. They travel there on weekends and for long vacations to relax and escape city life.

A group of cyclists rides through the countryside in the town of Brest. The French enjoy cycling as a pasttime to keep fit.

A man takes aim before rolling one of the metal balls in a game of boules in Provence.

Boules

Boules (BOOL) is a popular game in southern France. It is played with small, metal balls. Each player rolls a ball towards a smaller one, the *cochonnet* (ko-cho-NAY). The player whose ball lands closest to the cochonnet wins the game.

Sports

Soccer is probably the most popular sport in France. In 1998, France hosted and won the World Cup, beating the favorite, Brazil, in the final. In 2002, it was the runner-up.

Individual sports, such as skiing, cycling, and horseriding, are popular, too. The Alps provide some of the best ski slopes in the world. The Tour de France, the biggest cycling event of the year, covers more than 2,400 miles (3,862 kilometers).

Every year the best cyclists in the world take part in the Tour de France.

The French Alps are popular with skiers.

Carnival is a festival of parades, color, and costumes. It is the time of celebration before Lent.

Festivals

Many festivals take place throughout the year in France. The biggest are the Christian celebrations of Christmas and Easter. On January 6, or Twelfth Night, children celebrate Epiphany. A special pastry containing a surprise—usually a bean or pea—is served. The child who receives the surprise is made king or queen for the day. Just before Lent (the forty-day period of fasting before Easter), Carnival is celebrated.

Bastille Day

Bastille Day falls on July 14. It marks the beginning of the French Revolution and is celebrated as France's national day. The Tricolor flag flies in every city and town, and fireworks light up the night skies.

A dramatic fireworks display illuminates the Eiffel Tower in Paris on Bastille Day.

Festival de Cournouaille

Every year in July, the streets of Brittany are filled with Celtic culture. There are puppet shows, lace-making demonstrations, wrestling matches, and dancing. This is the Festival de Cournouaille, when Bretons celebrate their Celtic roots.

Avignon Festival

The Avignon Festival, France's largest arts festival, takes place during July and August. During this period, the town of Avignon comes alive with music and dancing. The festival has been held every year since it was founded by well-known French actors Gérard Philipe and Jean Vilar in 1947.

The people of Saint-Tropez, a town on France's Mediterranean coast, celebrate the Bravades Festival in May in honor of their patron saint and their military past.

Vendanges

Each September, grape harvest festivals, called *vendanges* (von-DAHNGES), celebrate the year's new wines. Many people enjoy wine tasting and folk dancing. The most important vendanges take place in Burgundy.

Food

France is famous for its delicious cuisine, and French food is served in restaurants all over the world. Each region in France has a special dish. *Bouillabaisse* (boo-yah-BES) is a rich seafood stew from the Mediterranean coast. *Ratatouille*, from Provence, is a vegetable dish made with herbs and olive oil. Along the Atlantic coast, fresh oysters, served raw or cooked, are a favorite.

Bread is so important to the French that the law requires each town or village to have a bakery selling fresh bread every day.

The French love to sit in outdoor cafés and enjoy a meal or a snack in the fresh air.

Family Meals

A popular breakfast in France consists of a *croissant* (CWAH-son)—a rich, flaky pastry—served with a large cup of coffee or hot chocolate.

Sunday lunch is the biggest meal of the week. The entire family gathers at home for a three-course meal of soup, roast meat, and a rich dessert. During the week, most people have a light lunch. The main meal of the day is dinner in the evening.

FRANCE

ENGLAND

NETHERLANDS

NORTH SEA

BELGIUM

LUXEMBOURG

Lille
NORD-PAS-DE-CALAIS

English Channel

UPPER NORMANDY

PICARDIE

LORRAINE

LOWER NORMANDY

Versailles ■ PARIS
ÎLE-DE-FRANCE

CHAMPAGNE-ARDENNE

Domrémy

BRITTANY

PAYS DE LA LOIRE

Seine

Orléans

CENTRE

Dijon

FRANCHE-COMTÉ

Loire

BURGUNDY

ATLANTIC OCEAN

POITOU-CHARENTES

LIMOUSIN

Vichy

Lyon

Mont Blanc
(15,771 feet/
4,808 meters)

Bay of Biscay

AUVERGNE

Massif Central

RHÔNE-ALPES

ALPS

Bordeaux
AQUITAINE

Rhône

MIDI-PYRÉNÉES

Avignon

PROVENCE-ALPES CÔTE-D'AZUR

Cannes

Marseille

Lourdes

PYRENEES

LANGUEDOC-ROUSSILLON

French Riviera

ANDORRA

SPAIN

MEDITERRANEAN SEA

	International Boundary
	State Boundary
■	Capital
●	City
▲	Mountain Peak
～	River

E

N

GERMANY

ALSACE

Rhine

SWITZERLAND

ITALY

MONACO

CORSICA

Alps D4
Alsace E2
Andorra C5
Aquitaine B4
Atlantic Ocean A3
Auvergne C3–C4
Avignon D4

Bay of Biscay A4
Belgium C1–D1
Bordeaux B4
Brittany A2–B2
Burgundy C3–D3

Cannes D4
Centre C2–C3
Champagne-Ardenne
    C2–D2
Corsica E5

Dijon D3
Domrémy D2

England B1
English Channel A2

Franche-Comté D3
French Riviera D5

Germany E1

Île-de-France C2
Italy E4

Languedoc-Roussillon
    C5
Lille C1
Limousin C3
Loire River B3
Lorraine D2
Lourdes B5
Lower Normandy B2

Luxembourg D1–D2
Lyon D3
Marseille D5
Massif Central C4
Mediterranean
    Sea D5
Midi-Pyrénées B5–C5
Monaco E4
Mont Blanc D3

Netherlands D1
Nord-Pas-de-Calais
    C1
North Sea C1

Orléans C2

Paris C2
Pays de la Loire B2–B3

Picardie C2
Poitou-Charentes B3
Provence-Alpes-Côte
    D'Azur D4
Pyrénées B5

Rhine River E2
Rhône-Alpes D3–D4
Rhône River D4

Seine River C2
Spain A5–C5
Switzerland E3

Upper Normandy
    B2–C2

Versailles C2
Vichy C3

A fountain at the Palace of Versailles.

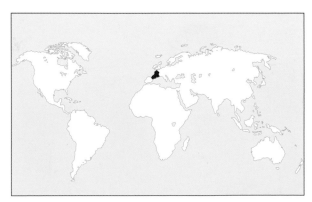

Quick Facts

Official Name   The French Republic

Capital   Paris

Official Language   French

Population   62,150,775 (July 2009 estimate)

Land Area   212,742 square miles (551,000 square kilometers)

Regions   Alsace, Aquitaine, Auvergne, Brittany, Burgundy, Centre, Champagne-Ardenne, Corsica, Franche-Comté, Île-de-France, Languedoc-Roussillon, Limousin, Lorraine, Lower Normandy, Midi-Pyrénées, Nord-Pas-de-Calais, Pays de la Loire, Picardie, Poitou-Charentes, Provence-Alpes-Côte d'Azur, Rhône-Alpes, Upper Normandy, overseas departments and territories

Highest Point   Mont Blanc 15,771 feet (4,805 meters)

Longest River   Loire River 634 miles (1,020 kilometers)

Main Religion   Roman Catholicism

National Anthem   *La Marseillaise* ("The Song of Marseille")

Currency   Euro (0.72 EUR = U.S. $1 in 2010)

The Hotel de Vogüé in Dijon. Many roofs there have beautiful tilework.

Glossary

allies: Nations that provide military and/or economic support for each other.

aristocracy: Members of the upper class, who have usually descended from nobility.

Breton: From Brittany or someone who lives in Brittany.

Celts: A group of people who originated in the British Isles.

cuisine: Food.

democratically: According to the principles of a system of government that is for the people and by the people.

demonstrations: Public displays of the attitudes of certain groups towards certain political or social issues.

dialect: Regional variety of a particular language.

European Union: A group of European countries that promotes free trade.

Gothic: A style of architecture popular in Europe from the twelfth to the sixteenth centuries.

immigrants: People who move to a country that is different from the one in which they were born.

literacy rate: The percentage of people who can read and write.

lycée: High school.

Middle Ages: The period in European history from about 500 to 1500 CE.

monarchy: A country or government ruled by a king or queen.

plateau: A large area of flat land that is higher than the surrounding areas.

Reformation: The sixteenth-century movement in Europe that split the Catholic Church into the Catholic and Protestant churches.

reforms: Changes that improve a particular system.

Renaissance: The movement in Europe between the fifteenth and seventeenth centuries that revived interest in literature and the arts and produced a creative flowering.

republic: A country in which supreme power rests with the people, who elect representatives to govern.

suburbs: Residential districts that are outside the city limits.

treason: The act of betraying a ruler, government, or country.

For More Information

Books

Brooks, Susie. *Let's Visit France*. New York: PowerKids Press, 2009.

Crosbie, Duncan. *Find Out About France: Learn French Words and Phrases and About Life in France*. New York: Barron's Educational Series, 2006.

Maceachern, Ashley. *Lance in France*. London: Collins, 2008.

Nardo, Don. *France*. Danbury, CT: Children's Press, 2007.

Streissguth, Tom. *France*. Minneapolis, MN: Lerner Classroom, 2008.

Tidmarsh, Celia. *France*. North Mankato, MN: Sea to Sea Publications, 2009.

DVDs

Discovery Atlas: France Revealed. (Discovery Channel, 2008).

Europe to the Max: Hidden Treasures—Splendors of France. (Questar, 2006).

Families of France. (Master Communications, 2006).

Globe-Toddlers Adventures in France!. (Tot Talk, Inc., 2006).

Globe Trekker: France & Paris. (Pilot Productions, 2005).

Websites

www.discoverfrance.net/France/Paris/Monuments-Paris/Eiffel.shtml
Contains a wealth of information about the culture, history, language of France, with a handy drop-down menu that offers a list of various topics.

www.oxfam.org.uk/coolplanet/ontheline/explore/journey/france/frindex.htm
Embark on a virtual journey through France and discover more about the country's lifestyle, culture, and more.

www.travelforkids.com/Funtodo/France/france.htm
Offers a snapshot of several French regions and cities, including Paris and Brittany. Also includes suggested books for further reading for children.

www.teacher.scholastic.com/activities/globaltrek/destinations/France.htm
Learn about France and its people on this site.

Index